★ THE ★
UNITED
STATES
PRESIDENTS

ELECTION 2020:
A LESSON IN CIVICS

Bailey J. Russell

Checkerboard Library

An Imprint of Abdo Publishing
abdobooks.com

ABDOBOOKS.COM

Published by Abdo Publishing, a division of ABDO, PO Box 398166, Minneapolis, Minnesota 55439. Copyright © 2021 by Abdo Consulting Group, Inc. International copyrights reserved in all countries. No part of this book may be reproduced in any form without written permission from the publisher. Checkerboard Library™ is a trademark and logo of Abdo Publishing.

Printed in the United States of America, North Mankato, Minnesota
012021
012021

THIS BOOK CONTAINS RECYCLED MATERIALS

Design: Emily O'Malley, Kelly Doudna, Mighty Media, Inc.
Production: Mighty Media, Inc.
Editors: Elizabeth Andrews, Tamara L. Britton, Tyler Gieseke

Cover Photographs: Morry Gash/POOL/EPA-EFE/Shutterstock; Patrick Semansky/AP/Shutterstock
Interior Photographs: aristotoo/iStock p. 32; Chip Somodevilla/Pool via AP p. 5; Christopher Penler/Shutterstock.com p. 39; DNCC/EPA-EFE/Shutterstock p. 11; DoraDalton/iStock p. 29; Jeff Kowalsky/Getty Images p. 14; LaMarr McDaniel/Shutterstock.com p. 38; Library of Congress pp. 40, 42; logolis/iStock p. 27; Morry Gash/POOL/EPA-EFE/Shutterstock, p 6; mpi04/MediaPunch /IPX p. 13; Olivier Douliery/Abaca (Sipa via AP Images) p. 36; Patrick Semansky/AP/Shutterstock p 6; REUTERS/Alamy Stock Photo p. 9; SAUL LOEB/UPI/Shutterstock p. 7; SDI Productions/iStock p. 26; Sharkstock/Shutterstock.com p. 6; Tom Williams/CQ Roll Call via AP Images pp. 7, 17; White House p. 44; Wikimedia Commons pp. 40, 42; Sipa USA/Alamy Live News p. 7; Brian Branch Price/ZUMA Wire/Alamy Live News p. 19

Library of Congress Control Number: 2020949910

Publisher's Cataloging-in-Publication Data
Names: Russell, Bailey J., author.
Title: Election 2020: a lesson in civics/ by Bailey J. Russell
Other title: a lesson in civics
Description: Minneapolis, Minnesota : Abdo Publishing, 2021 | Series: The United States presidents | Includes online resources and index.
Identifiers: ISBN 9781532195914 (lib. bdg.) | ISBN 9781098216658 (ebook)
Subjects: LCSH: Presidents--United States--Election--History--Juvenile literature. | Presidents--Juvenile literature. | Civics--Juvenile literature. | Legislators--United States--Juvenile literature. | Politics and government--Juvenile literature.
Classification: DDC 324.973--dc23

★ CONTENTS ★

Election 2020

The 2020 presidential election was like no other. A global **pandemic** caused many people to vote by mail. There was record voter turnout. And a mob broke into the Capitol building to protest what it saw as election **fraud**.

Republican candidate President Donald Trump was finishing a stormy first term. He had many accomplishments, such as historic peace treaties in the **Middle East**. But his campaign was investigated for **collusion** with another nation. And he became the first US president to be **impeached** twice.

Democratic candidate Joe Biden had served as vice president in former president Barack Obama's **administration**. He also had many career accomplishments. But there were concerns about his mental health. And he was suspected of questionable business dealings with foreign governments.

Election Day was November 3. But there was no clear winner on that day. In the coming weeks, the results of the election would be contested in many states. The fight eventually reached the highest court in the land.

Trump (*left*) and Biden debate at Belmont University in Nashville, Tennessee.

August 20, 2020

Joe Biden accepts the Democratic nomination for president.

August 24

Donald Trump accepts the Republican nomination.

December 8

Texas files a lawsuit in the Supreme Court against Michigan, Pennsylvania, Wisconsin, and Georgia; three days later, the court dismisses the suit.

November 7

The Associated Press calls the election for Joe Biden.

November 3

Election Day

December 14

Members of the electoral college meet to cast their votes.

January 20

Joe Biden is inaugurated the forty-sixth president of the United States; Kamala Harris is inaugurated the first female vice president.

January 6, 2021

A joint session of Congress meets to count and certify the electoral votes; a march outside the Capitol in support of President Trump turns violent, five people die; Congress meets later and certifies the electoral votes for Biden.

January 13

The House of Representatives votes to impeach President Trump for incitement of insurrection; he becomes the first president in history to be impeached twice.

Contested Elections

There have been other presidential elections in US history that were not decided on Election Day. The election of 1800 was the first decided by the House of Representatives. There was no popular vote then. Thomas Jefferson and Aaron Burr each won 73 electoral votes. In the House, Jefferson won ten states to Burr's four.

The second election the House decided was in 1824. Andrew Jackson won the popular vote but not the majority of electoral votes. When the House voted, John Quincy Adams won with 13 states while Jackson won seven.

In the 1876 election, Rutherford B. Hayes won 165 electoral votes. Samuel Tilden won 184. A candidate needed 185 to win. People **disputed** the results in Louisiana, South Carolina, and Florida. Congress created an electoral commission to resolve the dispute. The group awarded these states' 20 electoral votes to Hayes.

Finally, the Supreme Court decided the outcome of the 2000 election. Al Gore won the popular vote over George W. Bush. But he did not win a majority of the 537 electoral votes. To win, a candidate needed 270 electoral votes.

Florida's results were too close to decide a winner. So, state law called for a machine recount of the ballots. This recount gave Bush the lead. But Gore asked for a hand recount. Bush claimed this was against the law. He filed a lawsuit to stop it. The Supreme Court agreed and gave Bush Florida's 25 electoral votes. He won with 271 votes.

George W. Bush *(right)* is not the only president who did not win the popular vote. This also happened in 1824, 1876, 1888, and 2016.

A Unique Situation

The 2020 race for the White House began on August 20. That day former vice president Joe Biden accepted the Democratic **nomination** for president. He chose California senator Kamala Harris as his **running mate**.

Four days later, President Donald Trump accepted the Republican party's nomination for president. His running mate was Vice President Mike Pence.

Both campaigns began taking their message to the people. But this campaign was different than any other. In December 2019, the world learned of a mysterious disease in Wuhan, China.

Dozens of people were ill in Wuhan. Doctors and scientists worked to discover the cause. In early January 2020, they announced that the disease was caused by a new **coronavirus** called SARS-CoV-2. The disease became known as COVID-19.

The first case of COVID-19 in the United States was reported on January 20 in Washington State. Within ten days, the country had several other cases. Soon, the virus spread across the world and became a **pandemic**.

Kamala Harris greets supporters on Zoom at the Democratic National Convention in Milwaukee, Wisconsin. Due to the pandemic, the 2020 national conventions were virtual.

The Election

Because of the **pandemic,** Biden conducted most of his campaign remotely. In video interviews he spoke about his views on issues such as climate change, racism, and health care.

Trump held in-person rallies. Supporters heard him speak about job creation, tax cuts, and COVID-19 vaccine development. But on October 2, he and the First Lady tested positive for COVID-19. The president went into **quarantine.** He stopped campaigning while he recovered.

There were three presidential **debates** scheduled. The first was on September 29, 2020, at Case Western Reserve University in Cleveland, Ohio. The second was canceled due to COVID-19. The third was October 22, 2020, at Belmont University in Nashville, Tennessee.

The pandemic also affected how citizens voted. Many believed that in-person voting would spread the disease. Also, many states had issued stay-at-home orders. So, officials urged Americans to vote early by mail. They set up locations where voters could drop off paper ballots.

More than 100 million Americans voted early. In all, they cast 156 million votes, more than in any other election in US history.

On November 3, 2020, Americans went to the polls. At the end of the day, there was no clear winner. Results in some states were too close to call. Other states were still counting ballots. Early figures seemed to indicate a Trump win. But in the coming days, a different picture **emerged**.

Supreme Court Challenge

On November 7, the Associated Press announced Joe Biden was president-elect. He and Kamala Harris began assembling transition teams and planning for Biden's **administration**. But in the following days, hundreds of **bipartisan** witnesses signed sworn **affidavits** under penalty of **perjury** claiming election **fraud**.

A witness testifies at a hearing in Michigan in support of the Trump campaign. In all, more than 80 court cases were filed in response to the results of the election.

Officials discounted claims of **fraud**. But President Trump believed the claims should be investigated. To this end, the Trump campaign assembled a legal team. Independent lawyers also joined in.

Witnesses claimed they had seen fraudulent ballots and that some ballots had been counted more than once. Others claimed that voters' signatures on the ballots did not match the signatures on file. Some also claimed that software in vote-counting machines assigned votes cast for Trump to Biden's total.

In addition, the states of Georgia, Michigan, Pennsylvania, and Wisconsin had changed voting rules through their judicial and executive branches rather than through their legislative branches. On December 8, 2020, the state of Texas filed a lawsuit in the Supreme Court against these states. It alleged that these changes were unconstitutional and affected the votes of law-abiding states.

Eighteen states filed **briefs** in support of Texas's lawsuit. But On December 11, the court declined to hear the case. It said Texas had no interest in how other states ran their elections. Three days later, the electoral college met and cast their votes.

Congress Weighs In

Allegations of **fraud** continued. On January 4, 2021, a Wisconsin representative introduced a **resolution**. It said many citizens questioned the **integrity** of the elections due to election officials' failure to follow the law. It asked for **redress** of these **grievances**.

That same day, members of the Pennsylvania Senate asked that Vice President Pence delay certification of the electoral college votes until the Supreme Court heard a pending Trump campaign lawsuit against Pennsylvania's **secretary of state**. Then, on January 5, a US senator from South Carolina announced he would introduce a bill establishing a commission to improve the security and integrity of US federal elections.

On January 6, Congress met to count and certify the electoral college votes. Due to **fraud** claims, six senators and 121 representatives planned objections to some states' votes. Congress counts the states' electoral college votes in alphabetical order. When it came time to count Arizona's votes, one of the senators challenged the vote. Senators and representatives **adjourned** to **debate**.

Texas senator Ted Cruz (*center, in purple tie*) objects to Arizona's electoral votes in a joint session of Congress.

March Madness

President Trump strongly believed there had been fraud in the election. He asked supporters to attend a march in Washington, DC, while Congress counted the electoral votes. Thousands of people attended. The president gave a speech and encouraged protesters to walk to the Capitol building and protest there.

Protesters arrived at the Capitol and surrounded the building. Some began to push against the barricades that blocked its entrances. They fought with police and became violent. Eventually the crowd moved past the barricades and entered the building.

Congress called a **recess** and evacuated the building. Protesters vandalized doors and windows. Some went into congresspeople's offices and took things. In the **melee**, one woman was shot and killed. Four other people also died.

In response to the violence, the mayor of Washington, DC, ordered a 6 p.m. **curfew**. Congress met later that night. Just after 3 a.m., Vice President Mike Pence certified the electoral votes. Biden won with 306 votes over Trump's 232.

On January 6, Americans from across the nation gathered on the National Mall to support President Trump.

A New President

After the march, Congress condemned the actions of the protestors. Congressional challenges to the electoral vote count were abandoned. People accused President Trump of inciting a violent **insurrection**. Supporters said the president's speech at the march was peaceful. Accusers said Trump did not genuinely try to stop the violence.

On January 13, the House of Representatives voted to **impeach** the president for willful **incitement** of insurrection. It was the first time in American history that a president had been impeached twice.

On January 20, 2021, Joe Biden became the forty-sixth president of the United States. The people remained deeply divided over the results of the election. But America's systems of civics and government worked as they had for 276 years. Despite the challenges the 2020 presidential election posed, there was a peaceful transfer of power.

President Biden was 78 years old when he took office.
He was the oldest president in United States history.

★ A LESSON IN CIVICS ★

★ WHAT IS A VOTE?

A vote is a way for a citizen to choose a candidate for office.

★ HOW DOES THE VOTING PROCESS WORK?

 The voter goes to the polling place in his or her precinct to vote.

 Election workers give the voter a paper ballot.

 The voter goes to a voting booth and marks his or her choice on the ballot.

 The voter places his or her ballot into a voting machine.

 The voting machine counts all the ballots.

 Election officials make sure the voting results are right. They send them to their secretary of state.

 The secretary of state declares which candidate will receive the state's electoral votes.

 Federal election officials receive the voting results.

 State electors meet to cast their votes for president.

 The president of the US Senate reads the election results to Congress. Whoever receives the majority of the electoral votes wins the presidential election.

★ WHO CAN VOTE?

American citizens 18 years old or older can vote in national, state, and local elections. Each state decides the rules for voting in elections. But all states must follow the US Constitution's rules about voting. The US Constitution says that states cannot deny a citizen's right to vote based on race, color, or sex. The right to vote is one of an American citizen's most important rights. By voting, citizens directly affect the actions of their government.

★ VOTING ★

★ WHO IS AN AMERICAN CITIZEN?

A person born in the US.

A person born to US citizens living or traveling in foreign countries.

A person born in a foreign country who has become a naturalized citizen.

★ WHO IS A NATURALIZED CITIZEN?

A naturalized citizen is someone from another country who becomes an American citizen. A person becomes a naturalized citizen by filling out an application and passing a citizenship test.

★ WHAT IS A BALLOT?

A ballot is a device used to cast a vote. A vote may be cast by paper ballot, by voting machine, by computer punch card, or by computer. Citizens who are ill, physically disabled, or away from home can use an absentee ballot to vote. An absentee ballot is obtained from a local, county, or city election office.

★ WHAT IS A POLLING PLACE?

A polling place is where people go to vote. Public buildings like schools or community centers are often used as polling places.

★ WHAT IS THE POPULAR VOTE?

The popular vote is the total vote from all the states. It is made by citizens who are registered to vote.

★ WHAT IS A CANDIDATE?

A candidate is a person who runs for political office.

★ HOW IS A CANDIDATE CHOSEN?

In every presidential election, many candidates run for president. Some belong to the same political party. But each party can have only one candidate in the presidential election.

★ 1 ★ The political parties hold primaries or caucuses in each state.

★ 2 ★ Each primary and caucus chooses a candidate. Often, many different candidates are chosen.

★ 3 ★ The chosen candidates travel throughout the country. They make public appearances and give speeches.

★ 4 ★ Each party holds a national convention. There, each chooses one candidate from the primary and caucus winners to represent it in the presidential election.

★ WHAT IS A PRIMARY?

A primary is an election. In most primaries, political party members of a state vote for candidates from their party. In some primaries, citizens don't have to be party members to vote.

★ WHAT IS A CAUCUS?

A caucus is a meeting of political party leaders. In a caucus, party leaders of a state choose a candidate from their party.

★ WHAT IS A POLITICAL PARTY?

A political party is a group of people with similar political ideas. They try to put their ideas into action by electing a party member to the government. Anyone can form a political party. But not all parties are included on a state's presidential ballot. To get its candidate's name on a ballot, a party must often have thousands of members.

★ WHAT ARE THE MAIN POLITICAL PARTIES IN AMERICA?

There are many political parties in America. But the Republican and Democratic parties have been the main parties since the 1860s. Most Americans call themselves Republican or Democrat. Republicans favor a small government. Democrats favor a larger government. Every president since 1856 has been either a Republican or a Democrat. Since World War II ended, Republican and Democratic candidates have received almost all of the votes in the presidential elections.

"However [political parties] may now and then answer popular ends, they are likely in the course of time and things, to become potent engines, by which cunning, ambitious, and unprincipled men will be enabled to subvert the power of the people and to usurp for themselves the reins of government, destroying afterwards the very engines which have lifted them to unjust dominion."

PRESIDENT GEORGE WASHINGTON
Farewell Address - Saturday, September 17, 1796

★ WHAT IS AN ELECTION?

An election is the process of choosing a candidate by voting.

★ HOW DOES THE PRESIDENTIAL ELECTION WORK?

The US Constitution states that a presidential election is to be held every four years. It must be held on the Tuesday after the first Monday in November. In a presidential election, people do not vote directly for a presidential candidate. Instead, they vote for a group of people known as electors.

People in line to vote

These electors are part of the electoral college. They are supposed to vote for the candidate who wins the state's popular vote. By winning a state, the candidate receives all the state's electoral votes. When the election is over, Congress totals each candidate's electoral votes. The candidate who receives the majority of electoral votes wins the presidency.

★ WHAT IS AN ELECTOR?

An elector is a member of the US electoral college. The US Constitution says that state legislatures can choose their electors. Their number must equal the number of the state's members in Congress. Candidates for elector are often chosen at party conventions, in primary elections, or by party organizations. Officers of the federal government cannot be electors.

ELECTORAL COLLEGE

★ HOW DOES THE ELECTORAL COLLEGE WORK?

The electoral college is the system used to elect the president and vice president. The Founding Fathers created it so that both Congress and citizens have a role in the presidential election.

1
Political parties in each state appoint electors. Each state gets one elector for each senator and representative it has in Congress. Each elector has one electoral vote.

2
On the Tuesday after the first Monday in November, the citizens of each state cast a popular vote for president.

3
The candidate who wins a state's popular vote typically gets all the state's electoral votes.

4
On the Monday after the second Wednesday in December, each state's electors cast their votes for their state's winning candidate. Then they send the votes to Congress.

5
On the sixth day of January the following year, Congress counts the states' electoral votes. The president of the Senate announces the winner.

6
The new president is inaugurated on January 20.

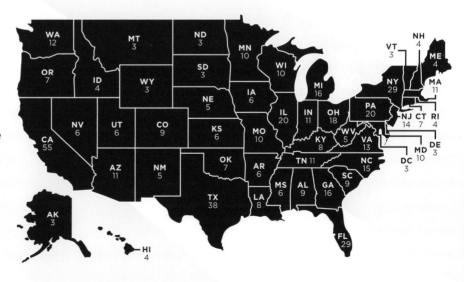

★ COURTS ★

★ WHAT IS A COURT?

A court is a place were legal cases are decided or where trials are held.

★ WHAT DO COURTS DO?

Courts use the law to settle disagreements between people, between people and the government, and between governments. Courts decide in favor of one side or another. The losing side can ask for a new trial from a higher court. This is called an appeal. A court decision can be appealed all the way to the US Supreme Court. It is the highest court in America. Once the Supreme Court makes a decision, it is final. No more appeals can be made.

★ HOW DOES THE COURT SYSTEM WORK?

Overall, there are 51 court systems in the US. There is one system for each state and one for the federal government. Federal courts work with state courts. Federal courts deal with cases involving constitutional law. State courts deal with cases involving their own constitution.

★ WHAT IS A LAWSUIT?

A lawsuit is a case in a court of law. Lawsuits are started by one person to claim something from another. Lawsuits are filed in courts, often by lawyers.

★ WHAT IS A LAWYER?

A lawyer is a person who knows the law. A lawyer gives advice about matters of law or acts for others in a court of law.

THE US COURT SYSTEM

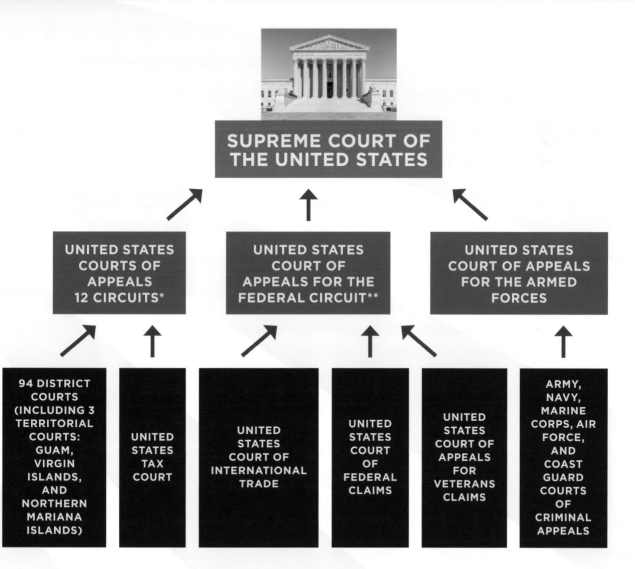

SUPREME COURT OF THE UNITED STATES

UNITED STATES COURTS OF APPEALS 12 CIRCUITS*

UNITED STATES COURT OF APPEALS FOR THE FEDERAL CIRCUIT**

UNITED STATES COURT OF APPEALS FOR THE ARMED FORCES

94 DISTRICT COURTS (INCLUDING 3 TERRITORIAL COURTS: GUAM, VIRGIN ISLANDS, AND NORTHERN MARIANA ISLANDS)

UNITED STATES TAX COURT

UNITED STATES COURT OF INTERNATIONAL TRADE

UNITED STATES COURT OF FEDERAL CLAIMS

UNITED STATES COURT OF APPEALS FOR VETERANS CLAIMS

ARMY, NAVY, MARINE CORPS, AIR FORCE, AND COAST GUARD COURTS OF CRIMINAL APPEALS

* The 12 regional courts of appeals also receive cases from a number of federal agencies.

** The Court of Appeals for the Federal Circuit also receives cases from the International Trade Commission, the Merit Systems Protection Board, the Patent and Trademark Office, and the Board of Contract Appeals.

★ WHAT IS A GOVERNMENT?

A government is a group of people who use laws to run a country, state, county, district, city, or town. In the United States, there are federal, state, and local governments.

★ WHAT IS THE FEDERAL GOVERNMENT?

The US Constitution describes the structure of the federal government. The federal government is the main government of the United States. It was formed to help the country run better and protect its citizens. The US Constitution divides the federal government into the executive, legislative, and judicial branches.

★ WHAT IS A STATE GOVERNMENT?

A state government is a group of people, organizations, and laws in charge of a state. State governments have all powers not given to the federal government by the US Constitution. Each state uses its own constitution as the basis for its laws. All state constitutions are different. That's because each state has its own history, needs, beliefs, and geography. Each state's constitution is similar to the US Constitution. All state constitutions must obey the laws in the US Constitution. Each state's constitution separates power into three branches: executive, legislative, and judicial. In all states except one, the legislative branch has a senate and a house of representatives. In Nebraska, the state legislature only has one house.

★ WHY DOES AMERICA HAVE STATES?

America was once made up of thirteen colonies ruled by Great Britain. In 1776, the colonies declared their independence. After the colonies won the Revolutionary War, they became states. Each state formed its own government. A federal government was created when the states ratified the US Constitution in 1787.

GOVERNMENT

THESE ARE THE THINGS ONLY THE FEDERAL GOVERNMENT CAN DO:

- ★ Decide how to treat other countries.
- ★ Declare war.
- ★ Have an army and navy.
- ★ Make treaties.
- ★ Oversee business between states and other countries.
- ★ Print money.
- ★ Run post offices.

THESE ARE THE THINGS ONLY THE STATE GOVERNMENTS CAN DO:

- ★ Carry out public health and safety actions.
- ★ Form local governments.
- ★ Give out licenses.
- ★ Hold elections.
- ★ Oversee business in the state.
- ★ Ratify amendments to the US Constitution.

★ WHAT IS A LOCAL GOVERNMENT?

A local government is a group of people, organizations, and laws in charge of a county, city, town, or district. Local governments get their powers from their state's constitution. Most Americans live under several local governments. There are five forms of local government.

★ WHAT IS A PRECINCT?

A precinct is a part of a county, city, town, or district. But it does not have its own government. Precincts are formed to help organize an area for voting and police protection.

LOCAL GOVERNMENT

COUNTY
- ★ OFTEN THE LARGEST UNIT OF LOCAL GOVERNMENT. MOST STATES, EXCEPT CONNECTICUT AND RHODE ISLAND, ARE DIVIDED INTO COUNTIES.

TOWNSHIP
- ★ A SMALLER UNIT OF A COUNTY. TOWNSHIPS ARE THE LEAST COMMON FORM OF LOCAL GOVERNMENT IN AMERICA.

MUNICIPALITY
- ★ AREAS THAT ARE INCORPORATED AND OFTEN INCLUDE CITIES.

SPECIAL DISTRICT
- ★ THE MOST COMMON LOCAL GOVERNMENT IN AMERICA. THEY ARE FORMED TO MEET SPECIAL NEEDS OF AN AREA, LIKE FARMLAND.

SCHOOL DISTRICT
- ★ AN AREA THAT PROVIDES LOCAL SCHOOLS. A BOARD OF EDUCATION OVERSEES A SCHOOL DISTRICT.

★ WHAT IS A CONSTITUTION?

A constitution is a written plan for government. It says how a country or state's government will be organized. America and all its states have constitutions.

★ WHAT IS THE US CONSTITUTION?

The US Constitution describes the structure of the federal government and the rights of the American people. The US Constitution also includes the Bill of Rights.

The US Constitution

★ WHAT IS THE BILL OF RIGHTS?

The Bill of Rights is the first ten amendments to the US Constitution. It gives citizens certain freedoms and rights, including the right to vote.

★ WHAT IS AN AMENDMENT?

An amendment is a change to the Constitution. A member of Congress proposes the amendment. Two-thirds of each house of Congress must approve a proposed amendment, and three-fourths of the states must ratify it.

★ LAWS ★

★ WHAT IS A LAW?

A law is a rule made by a country or state to protect its citizens.

★ WHO MAKES LAWS?

Congress makes laws. A law begins as a bill. A bill is a written idea for a new law. Bills can be introduced in the House of Representatives or the Senate. When a bill is approved, it becomes a law. If a bill begins in the House, representatives vote on it first. If it passes, the bill goes to the Senate for approval. If a bill begins in the Senate, senators vote on it first. If it passes, the bill goes to the House for approval. A bill can die at any point in this process. A bill dies when not enough congresspeople vote in favor of it. A bill can die in a committee, in the House, or in the Senate.

★ HOW DOES A BILL BECOME A LAW?

★ 1 ★

A bill is introduced in either the House of Representatives or the Senate.

The bill goes to a committee for review. Sometimes, it makes changes to the bill.

The committee sends the bill back to the House of Representatives or the Senate for debate. Then they vote on it.

★ 2 ★

If approved, the bill is sent to the opposite chamber of Congress.

The bill goes to a committee for review. Sometimes, it makes changes to the bill.

The committee sends the bill back to the House of Representatives or the Senate. Then they vote on it.

If approved, the bill goes to a committee of House and Senate members. They meet to agree on final changes to the bill.

★ 3 ★

Congress sends the bill to the president, who studies it.

THE BILL BECOMES A LAW IF:
- The president signs it.
- The president does not sign it for ten days while Congress is in session.
- Two-thirds of Congress votes in favor of the bill.

THE BILL DOES NOT BECOME A LAW IF:
- The president vetoes it. If vetoed, the bill goes back to Congress. The Senate and the House vote on the bill again.
- The president does not sign it for ten days while Congress is not in session.

BRANCHES OF GOVERNMENT

The US government is divided into three branches. They are the executive, legislative, and judicial branches. This division is called a separation of powers. Each branch has some power over the others. This is called a system of checks and balances.

★ EXECUTIVE BRANCH

The executive branch enforces laws. It is made up of the president, the vice president, and the president's cabinet. The president represents the United States around the world. He or she oversees relations with other countries and signs treaties. The president signs bills into law and appoints officials and federal judges. He or she also leads the military and manages government workers.

★ LEGISLATIVE BRANCH

The legislative branch makes laws, maintains the military, and regulates trade. It also has the power to declare war. This branch consists of the Senate and the House of Representatives. Together, these two houses make up Congress. Each state has two senators. A state's population determines the number of representatives it has.

★ JUDICIAL BRANCH

The judicial branch interprets laws. It consists of district courts, courts of appeals, and the Supreme Court. District courts try cases. If a person disagrees with a trial's outcome, he or she may appeal. If a court of appeals supports the ruling, a person may appeal to the Supreme Court. The Supreme Court also makes sure that laws follow the US Constitution.

THE PRESIDENT ★

★ QUALIFICATIONS FOR OFFICE

To be president, a person must meet three requirements. A candidate must be at least 35 years old and a natural-born US citizen. He or she must also have lived in the United States for at least 14 years.

★ ELECTORAL COLLEGE

The US presidential election is an indirect election. Voters from each state choose electors to represent them in the Electoral College. The number of electors from each state is based on the state's population. Each elector has one electoral vote. Electors are pledged to cast their vote for the candidate who receives the highest number of popular votes in their state. A candidate must receive the majority of Electoral College votes to win.

★ TERM OF OFFICE

Each president may be elected to two four-year terms. Sometimes, a president may only be elected once. This happens if he or she served more than two years of the previous president's term.

The presidential election is held on the Tuesday after the first Monday in November. The president is sworn in on January 20 of the following year. At that time, he or she takes the oath of office:

> *I do solemnly swear (or affirm) that I will faithfully execute the office of President of the United States, and will to the best of my ability, preserve, protect and defend the Constitution of the United States.*

★ LINE OF SUCCESSION ★

The Presidential Succession Act of 1947 defines who becomes president if the president cannot serve. The vice president is first in the line of succession. Next are the Speaker of the House and the President Pro Tempore of the Senate. If none of these individuals is able to serve, the office falls to the president's cabinet members. They would take office in the order in which each department was created:

Secretary of State

Secretary of the Treasury

Secretary of Defense

Attorney General

Secretary of the Interior

Secretary of Agriculture

Secretary of Commerce

Secretary of Labor

Secretary of Health and Human Services

Secretary of Housing and Urban Development

Secretary of Transportation

Secretary of Energy

Secretary of Education

Secretary of Veterans Affairs

Secretary of Homeland Security

While in office, the president receives a salary of $400,000 each year. He or she lives in the White House and has 24-hour Secret Service protection.

The president may travel on a Boeing 747 jet called Air Force One. The airplane can accommodate 76 passengers. It has kitchens, a dining room, sleeping areas, and a conference room. It also has fully equipped offices with the latest communications systems. Air Force One can fly halfway around the world before needing to refuel. It can even refuel in flight!

Air Force One

If the president wishes to travel by car, he or she uses Cadillac One. It has been modified with heavy armor and communications systems. The president takes

Cadillac One along when visiting other countries if secure transportation will be needed.

The president also travels on a helicopter called Marine One. Like the presidential car, Marine One accompanies the president when traveling abroad if necessary.

Cadillac One

Sometimes, the president needs to get away and relax with family and friends. Camp David is the official presidential retreat. It is located in the cool, wooded mountains of Maryland. The US Navy maintains the retreat, and the US Marine Corps keeps it secure. The camp offers swimming, tennis, golf, and hiking.

When the president leaves office, he or she receives lifetime Secret Service protection. He or she also receives a yearly pension of $207,800 and funding for office space, supplies, and staff.

Marine One

	PRESIDENT	PARTY	TOOK OFFICE
1	George Washington	None	April 30, 1789
2	John Adams	Federalist	March 4, 1797
3	Thomas Jefferson	Democratic-Republican	March 4, 1801
4	James Madison	Democratic-Republican	March 4, 1809
5	James Monroe	Democratic-Republican	March 4, 1817
6	John Quincy Adams	Democratic-Republican	March 4, 1825
7	Andrew Jackson	Democrat	March 4, 1829
8	Martin Van Buren	Democrat	March 4, 1837
9	William H. Harrison	Whig	March 4, 1841
10	John Tyler	Whig	April 6, 1841
11	James K. Polk	Democrat	March 4, 1845
12	Zachary Taylor	Whig	March 5, 1849
13	Millard Fillmore	Whig	July 10, 1850
14	Franklin Pierce	Democrat	March 4, 1853
15	James Buchanan	Democrat	March 4, 1857
16	Abraham Lincoln	Republican	March 4, 1861
17	Andrew Johnson	Democrat	April 15, 1865
18	Ulysses S. Grant	Republican	March 4, 1869
19	Rutherford B. Hayes	Republican	March 3, 1877

George Washington

Abraham Lincoln

Theodore Roosevelt

THEIR TERMS ★

LEFT OFFICE	TERMS SERVED	VICE PRESIDENT
March 4, 1797	Two	John Adams
March 4, 1801	One	Thomas Jefferson
March 4, 1809	Two	Aaron Burr, George Clinton
March 4, 1817	Two	George Clinton, Elbridge Gerry
March 4, 1825	Two	Daniel D. Tompkins
March 4, 1829	One	John C. Calhoun
March 4, 1837	Two	John C. Calhoun, Martin Van Buren
March 4, 1841	One	Richard M. Johnson
April 4, 1841	Died During First Term	John Tyler
March 4, 1845	Completed Harrison's Term	Office Vacant
March 4, 1849	One	George M. Dallas
July 9, 1850	Died During First Term	Millard Fillmore
March 4, 1853	Completed Taylor's Term	Office Vacant
March 4, 1857	One	William R.D. King
March 4, 1861	One	John C. Breckinridge
April 15, 1865	Served One Term, Died During Second Term	Hannibal Hamlin, Andrew Johnson
March 4, 1869	Completed Lincoln's Second Term	Office Vacant
March 4, 1877	Two	Schuyler Colfax, Henry Wilson
March 4, 1881	One	William A. Wheeler

	PRESIDENT	PARTY	TOOK OFFICE
20	James A. Garfield	Republican	March 4, 1881
21	Chester Arthur	Republican	September 20, 1881
22	Grover Cleveland	Democrat	March 4, 1885
23	Benjamin Harrison	Republican	March 4, 1889
24	Grover Cleveland	Democrat	March 4, 1893
25	William McKinley	Republican	March 4, 1897
26	Theodore Roosevelt	Republican	September 14, 1901
27	William Taft	Republican	March 4, 1909
28	Woodrow Wilson	Democrat	March 4, 1913
29	Warren G. Harding	Republican	March 4, 1921
30	Calvin Coolidge	Republican	August 3, 1923
31	Herbert Hoover	Republican	March 4, 1929
32	Franklin D. Roosevelt	Democrat	March 4, 1933
33	Harry S. Truman	Democrat	April 12, 1945
34	Dwight D. Eisenhower	Republican	January 20, 1953
35	John F. Kennedy	Democrat	January 20, 1961
36	Lyndon B. Johnson	Democrat	November 22, 1963

Franklin D. Roosevelt

John F. Kennedy

Ronald Reagan

LEFT OFFICE	TERMS SERVED	VICE PRESIDENT
September 19, 1881	Died During First Term	Chester Arthur
March 4, 1885	Completed Garfield's Term	Office Vacant
March 4, 1889	One	Thomas A. Hendricks
March 4, 1893	One	Levi P. Morton
March 4, 1897	One	Adlai E. Stevenson
September 14, 1901	Served One Term, Died During Second Term	Garret A. Hobart, Theodore Roosevelt
March 4, 1909	Completed McKinley's Second Term, Served One Term	Office Vacant, Charles Fairbanks
March 4, 1913	One	James S. Sherman
March 4, 1921	Two	Thomas R. Marshall
August 2, 1923	Died During First Term	Calvin Coolidge
March 4, 1929	Completed Harding's Term, Served One Term	Office Vacant, Charles Dawes
March 4, 1933	One	Charles Curtis
April 12, 1945	Served Three Terms, Died During Fourth Term	John Nance Garner, Henry A. Wallace, Harry S. Truman
January 20, 1953	Completed Roosevelt's Fourth Term, Served One Term	Office Vacant, Alben Barkley
January 20, 1961	Two	Richard Nixon
November 22, 1963	Died During First Term	Lyndon B. Johnson
January 20, 1969	Completed Kennedy's Term, Served One Term	Office Vacant, Hubert H. Humphrey

	PRESIDENT	PARTY	TOOK OFFICE
37	Richard Nixon	Republican	January 20, 1969
38	Gerald Ford	Republican	August 9, 1974
39	Jimmy Carter	Democrat	January 20, 1977
40	Ronald Reagan	Republican	January 20, 1981
41	George H.W. Bush	Republican	January 20, 1989
42	Bill Clinton	Democrat	January 20, 1993
43	George W. Bush	Republican	January 20, 2001
44	Barack Obama	Democrat	January 20, 2009
45	Donald Trump	Republican	January 20, 2017
46	Joe Biden	Democrat	January 20, 2021

Barack Obama

★ PRESIDENTS MATH GAME ★

Have fun with this presidents math game! First, study the list above and memorize each president's name and number. Then, use math to figure out which president completes each equation below.

1. Herbert Hoover + Franklin Pierce =?

2. Woodrow Wilson + Ulysses S. Grant=?

3. Franklin D. Roosevelt - Zachary Taylor=?

Answers: 1. Donald Trump (31+14=45)
2. Joe Biden (28+18=46)
3. James A. Garfield (32-12=20)

LEFT OFFICE	TERMS SERVED	VICE PRESIDENT
August 9, 1974	Completed First Term, Resigned During Second Term	Spiro T. Agnew, Gerald Ford
January 20, 1977	Completed Nixon's Second Term	Nelson A. Rockefeller
January 20, 1981	One	Walter Mondale
January 20, 1989	Two	George H.W. Bush
January 20, 1993	One	Dan Quayle
January 20, 2001	Two	Al Gore
January 20, 2009	Two	Dick Cheney
January 20, 2017	Two	Joe Biden
January 20, 2021	One	Mike Pence
		Kamala Harris

★ WRITE TO THE PRESIDENT ★

You may write to the president at:

**The White House
1600 Pennsylvania Avenue NW
Washington, DC 20500**

You may email the president at:

www.whitehouse.gov/contact

adjourn—to stop work until a later time.

administration—a group of people that manages an operation, a department, or an office.

affidavit—a sworn statement made under oath to tell the truth.

bipartisan—of, relating to, or involving members of two parties.

brief—a formal written argument.

collusion—a secret agreement or cooperation especially for an illegal or deceitful purpose.

coronavirus—any of a family of viruses that are studded with club-shaped spike proteins. These include viruses that cause the diseases MERS, SARS, and COVID-19.

curfew—a rule requiring a person to be home by a certain time.

debate—a contest in which two sides argue for or against something.

dispute—a forceful argument. To dispute something is to question it.

emerge—to come out into view.

fraud—an act of deceiving or misrepresenting. Something that has been subject to fraud is fraudulent.

grievance—a cause of distress.

impeach—to charge a public official with misconduct in office.

incite—to move to action.

insurrection—an act or instance of revolting against civil authority or an established government.

integrity—a firm adherence to a code of moral values.

melee—a hand-to-hand fight among several people.

Middle East—a region made up of the lands of southwestern Asia and northeastern Africa.

nominate—to propose as a candidate for election to office.

pandemic—worldwide spread of a disease that can affect most people.

perjury—telling a lie when under oath to tell the truth.

quarantine—the separation of people from others in order to stop a disease from spreading.

recess—a suspension of business or procedure.

redress—to set right or correct a wrong.

resolution—a formal expression of opinion, will, or intent voted by an official body or assembled group.

running mate—a candidate running for a lower-rank position on an election ticket, especially the candidate for vice president.

secretary of state—in Pennsylvania, the state's chief election official and keeper of the state's seal.

ONLINE RESOURCES

Booklinks
NONFICTION NETWORK
FREE! ONLINE NONFICTION RESOURCES

To learn more about Election 2020, please visit **abdobooklinks.com** or scan this QR code. These links are routinely monitored and updated to provide the most current information available.

★ INDEX ★